Original title:
Hats off to Adventure

Copyright © 2025 Creative Arts Management OÜ
All rights reserved.

Author: Mariana Leclair
ISBN HARDBACK: 978-1-80586-034-1
ISBN PAPERBACK: 978-1-80586-506-3

On the Edge of Wonder

With suitcase in hand and shoes untied,
I tripped on my laces, my ego defied.
A monkey now wears my favorite cap,
He's laughing it up, oh, what a mishap!

From mountains so high to rivers so wide,
I slipped on a banana, oh how I glide!
The world is a circus, and life's just a show,
With every odd tumble, my courage will grow.

Tales of Daring Wanderlust

I sailed on a ship made of jellybeans,
And danced with a fish in bright purple jeans.
My compass was spinning, I followed the wrong,
But ended up singing a very loud song!

A dragon on roller skates zoomed right past,
He winked and he giggled, said, 'You're a blast!'
With every wild tale, there's laughter to share,
In the land of the silly, adventure's laid bare.

A Journey in Every Stitch

My backpack is bursting with mismatched socks,
I found a new friend in a pair of old crocs.
Together we wandered through fields of lost dreams,
While chasing the sun, we laughed till it seems!

From knitting a sweater for a porcupine,
To baking a cake and adding some slime.
Every thread tells a story, each patch has a grin,
In this quirky adventure, let the fun begin!

The Unfolding Road

The road unravels like a colorful scarf,
I rode on a turtle who liked to disbarf.
With every odd bump, a new giggle ensues,
You wouldn't believe the things I might lose!

An odd parade comes with each twist and turn,
With marching band squirrels, it's hard not to yearn.
So here's to odd journeys, where fun has no end,
Each hiccup a treasure, and laughter our friend.

The Language of New Beginnings

When life hands you a chance to dance,
Grab your shoes and take a glance.
With a giggle and a twirl so grand,
Oh, look! A squirrel with a master plan.

Each step we take on unmarked ground,
Might lead us where joy can be found.
In sneakers or boots, our hearts beat loud,
Chasing the clouds, we're fearless and proud.

Steps into the Unknown

One toe in water, it's freezing still,
A leap of faith? Yes, that's the thrill.
We waddle like ducks, make quite the scene,
Splashing around like we're all seventeen.

Maps upside down, who needs a guide?
With laughter as fuel, we'll take it in stride.
Lost in the giggles, we might find gold,
Or a dog on a skateboard, just as foretold.

Where Curiosity Leads

Peeking around corners with a wink and a grin,
What wonders await, let the wild games begin!
From upside-down cakes to squirrels in suits,
The world is a stage, and we're all in cahoots.

With bubblegum clowns and balloons in the sky,
Every twist and turn makes our spirits fly high.
Following whims like a mischievous breeze,
We'll dance with the daisies, if you please!

A Tapestry of Trails

A path woven with laughter, a thread of delight,
Under the moon's glow, the stars shining bright.
With each step we take, the stories unfold,
Of jellybean wishes and secrets retold.

From puddle splashing to caramel trees,
Adventure awaits in the rustling leaves.
Let's spin in circles and chase after rain,
In a world of wonder, we're never mundane.

Boundless Frontiers Await

In the land of curious socks,
We dance with chickens in frocks.
Llamas strut with flair and glee,
Join the circus—come, just see!

Hot air balloons shaped like fries,
We fly through clouds, oh what a prize!
With kites shaped like giant fish,
We chase a daydream, make a wish!

Through mud puddles, we do leap,
In search of goats that can't stop sheep.
With sparkly capes and mismatched shoes,
It's not a race, but we'll never snooze!

A pirate crew of merry men,
We sail on bath toys time and again.
So buckle up, it's quite a ride,
In this kooky world, we all abide!

Quest for the Unseen

A steam-powered toaster goes for a spin,
With jam-fueled rockets, the race begins!
Invisible monsters, oh what a sight,
We battle them daily—well, just in the night!

With binoculars made from rolled-up news,
We search for treasures in old, worn shoes.
In a world where cookies reign supreme,
We munch and crunch — oh, what a dream!

Sailing on boats of paper and glue,
Navigating waters of jellybean blue.
When we find our way with snacks aglow,
Truth be told, we're just here for the show!

Dancing on rooftops, singing with flair,
In our search for mischief, we've no time to spare!
With a wink and a nod, we shatter the norm,
This quest for the unseen is quite the storm!

Footsteps into Tomorrow

In shoes that squeak with every stride,
We leap into tomorrows with silly pride.
With rainbow socks and wigs askew,
We step into moments both wild and new!

Puppies on scooters zooming by,
While we're off to chase the sky.
A treasure map drawn in crayon bright,
Leading us to fun from morning to night!

We twist and twirl on the wobbly ground,
Giggling loud with joy all around.
Each step a dance, each moment a song,
In this silly world, we all belong!

So pack your laughter, leave fears at the door,
With every adventure, we'll find even more.
Together we'll romp in this wondrous play,
With funny footsteps, we'll lead the way!

Whispers of the Wild

In a jungle of giggles, where tigers wear ties,
We wander through bushes, oh look, a surprise!
Monkeys in shades swinging high from the trees,
Sharing their secrets with butterflies and bees!

With coconuts rolling like bowling balls,
We kite surf on rainbows, heed nature's calls.
A land where the sun wears a goofy grin,
And clouds float by in a cotton candy spin!

The crickets are drummers, the frogs hold a show,
With sneaky raccoons joining in just for the glow.
Dancing through leaves to a whimsical beat,
In this wild wonderland, we skip and repeat.

So grab your sombrero, and let's hit the trail,
With laughter as our compass, we cannot fail!
In whispers of wild where adventures ignite,
We'll find the joy that makes everything bright!

The Compass of Curiosity

In a world where squirrels can fly,
A map in hand, we'll reach for the sky.
With monkey costumes and a pie in tow,
Let's set sail where the wild giggles grow.

Grab your shoes with squeaky soles,
We'll chase down laughter and belly rolls.
An octopus juggles, a llama will dance,
Join the parade, it's your chance to prance.

Sails of Serendipity

With a rubber duck as our trusty guide,
We'll surf the waves of the purple tide.
Coconuts laughing, trees in a spin,
Every twist and turn, let the fun begin.

Pirates with puppies, and tacos that sing,
Spinning in circles like a whirling spring.
Surprises abound on this wacky throne,
Sails of joy carrying us home.

Boundless Paths of Discovery

In a land where socks mysteriously flee,
We'll search for treasures beneath the tea tree.
A parade of ducks in hats made of cheese,
We'll dance as we wander, as wild as we please.

Hopping over puddles and wiggly worms,
Every corner hides giggles and squirms.
Join the fun, it's a crazed ballet,
With boundless paths where silliness plays.

Steps Into the Wild Unknown

With fireworks bursting in colors so bright,
We'll tiptoe lightly, keep hearts full of light.
A balding raccoon wearing shades of green,
Guides us through forests where laughter is seen.

Jellybean clouds float by in a rush,
Giggling frogs trigger a playful hush.
With each step we take, the world spins and twirls,
Into the wild unknown, laughter unfurls.

Echoes of the Untamed

In a field of cows I stood,
Waving my arms, like a hood.
They stared back, chewing away,
Wondering if I'd bring hay.

I danced like a deer, quite odd,
Startedle the farmer, oh God!
He chuckled and shook his head,
'What's wrong with this guy instead?'

A squirrel joined in my cheer,
With a nut, it showed no fear.
We pranced 'round the muddy mire,
Not caring much, it's our empire.

Under the sun, laughter soared,
Nature's stage, we both adored.
In wild delight, we found peace,
With friends like these, troubles cease.

Dreams on the Open Road

I jumped in my car, full of cheer,
With a map marked in bright, neon gear.
The GPS said, 'Turn right', oh dear!
I followed, and landed in someone's deer.

A llama crossed, in stolen shades,
As I made my way through winding glades.
It winked at me, so I gave a toot,
We shared a laugh, what a wild hoot!

Next, I hit a pizza parade,
Where zest and toppings happily played.
I yelled, 'No anchovies, not today!'
As slices flew—oh, what a fray!

With crust on my hat and cheese in my hair,
I zoomed off, no time to spare.
Chasing dreams on this bumpy ride,
Adventure awaits, let's take it in stride!

Chasing Sunsets and Stars

Out on the beach, I spotted a kite,
Struggling like me to reach new height.
I gave it a tug, it danced in the breeze,
Together we laughed at the gulls and the trees.

My friend rolled in with a grand big drum,
Said he'd summon the waves, beat the hum.
So we banged and we bopped till the stars all twinkled,
The fish flopped high, and the seagulls wrinkled.

We built a grand castle; it toppled so fast,
But we didn't mind, we were having a blast.
With sand in our shoes and salt in our hair,
We chased the horizon without a care.

As night cloaked the sky, we danced on the shore,
With laughter and joy, who could ask for more?
With dreams of the cosmos shining sublime,
We shouted our joy—let's have more fun time!

Beyond Familiar Shadows

In the woods, I took a bend,
And met a fox, my quirky friend.
He wore a tie, but lost his way,
Said, 'Help me find the end of the day!'

We tripped o'er roots and giggled, oh dear,
As he barked with laughter and danced with cheer.
He asked me, 'What's your name, good chap?'
But my only answer was a silly clap.

A bear joined in, with polka dots,
He spun around, ignoring the knots.
Together we made quite a circus show,
As tree trunks echoed our funny flow.

We stumbled through shadows, round and round,
In this playful realm where joy abounds.
With fables and laughter filling the air,
Life is the greatest adventure we share!

Embracing the Edge of the World

With a map made of crumpled dreams,
I set sail on coffee-fueled schemes.
Flip-flops on the edge of fate,
Waves of laughter shout, "Don't be late!"

Canoes transformed to flying boats,
My compass spins like a silly goat.
Lost in thought, I climb a tree,
A squirrel shakes his head at me.

An ice cream cone becomes my guide,
As birds of wisdom laugh and glide.
Chasing clouds that tease and race,
I trip on joy, a slapstick chase.

Oh, the world's a jester dressed in cheer,
With each misstep, the path grows clear.
At the edge, I embrace the fall,
With giggles echoing, I stand tall.

A Tapestry of Trails

Stitching paths with my mismatched socks,
I wander through fields with fencing blocks.
Tangled in vines, my spirit bursts,
Each leaf a mirror of silly thirsts.

A backpack filled with snacks and glee,
As I trip over roots that laugh at me.
With every tumble, my heart leaps high,
Squirrels in berets join my sky-high fly.

Footprints painted in ice cream swirls,
Chasing butterflies in soggy curls.
The trail of giggles, a path so sweet,
In every corner, another treat.

Through the tapestry of wild and free,
Every mishap draws a smiley spree.
Collecting laughs like flowers in bloom,
Adventure winks from every room.

Spirits of Adventurous Souls

With backpacks heavy, laughter light,
We wade through puddles, barefoot delight.
Each twist and turn, a dance of fate,
Socks on our hands, isn't that great?

An old map drawn in crayon hues,
Leads us to places with silly shoes.
We stumble and tumble, the world our stage,
The fizzy laughter fuels our age.

In fields of buttercups, we pirouette,
Chasing shadows we'll never forget.
Campfire stories, marshmallows collide,
Each silly tale a joyful ride.

Atop the hill, we serenade the moon,
With giggles echoing, life's a cartoon.
In the embrace of a starry scroll,
Adventurers dance, and we lose control.

Serene Steps in Unfamiliar Lands

Each step a whisper on foreign ground,
Where awkward greets the world profound.
My shoes converse in clumsy rhymes,
In lands where laughter unravels times.

A curious cat dons spectacles bright,
Guiding my path with whimsical might.
As I misread signs with a wink and a grin,
The universe chuckles, inviting me in.

With banana peels strewn on the track,
I take graceful tumbles, no need to backtrack.
Every stumble a dance, clumsy yet grand,
This world spins laughter, a merry band.

Through serene steps in a giggling trance,
Adventure unfolds in a silly dance.
Embracing the quirks, it's plain to see,
In every misstep, I'm wild and free.

A Journey with No End

With a backpack and a grin,
We march towards the bright unknown,
Maps upside down, we spin,
While laughter's wild winds have grown.

Each step a dance, a twist, a shout,
The road is long but full of cheer,
Where wonders bloom and doubts are out,
As every turn brings silly fear.

A stumble here, a laugh erupts,
Each misstep leads to joy unplanned,
We chase the sun, no time for interrupts,
While dreams parade, hand in hand.

With gnomes and trolls, the tales collide,
We break the rules of what is meant,
For life's a ride, we'll not divide,
A journey where our hearts are lent.

Emblazoned by Adventure

In a car that's barely run,
With snacks and tunes, we hit the trail,
Our laughter shines, we're having fun,
A journey where we'll never pale.

With maps that point to 'Not a clue',
We venture forth, through mud and rain,
Each pothole marks a tale or two,
As stories grow, we entertain.

We chase the light, we dodge the gloom,
In every nook, a surprise we find,
From rooftops high to tiny rooms,
Adventure's spark ignites our mind.

When all seems lost, we break out laughing,
For life's a script that's never done,
Entranced by chaos, we're crafting,
A tapestry of endless fun.

Navigating Dreams in Midnight Black

In the dark with moonlit beams,
We sail through dreams, oh what a sight,
With stars to guide our silly schemes,
As shadows dance in pure delight.

Each gust of wind, a joke in tow,
We wade through puddles, splash, and squeal,
With every turn, our laughter grows,
As night reveals its playful zeal.

Maps are scribbled, paths are bent,
In twilight's grip, we lose our way,
Yet joy erupts, our hearts are spent,
In midnight black, we choose to play.

With friends like stars, bright in our minds,
Navigating life's sweet chaos,
No rules to bind, just giggles and finds,
Adventure calls, we're surely tossed.

The Lure of the Horizon

Oh, the horizon is calling,
With colors that spin and sway,
It teases us, over hills, sprawling,
We chase its gaze, come what may.

With snacks galore and music loud,
An impromptu dance on grassy plains,
We make our own, raucous crowd,
As silliness pours like summer rains.

A tumble here, a wild caper,
We laugh until all breath is spent,
With every sun, a new paper,
Of stories shared, our hearts content.

The lure of distant lands, so bright,
Awaits the brave who choose to roam,
In whimsical tales, we take flight,
For every step, we find our home.

A Canvas of Possibilities

A quirky cat with a curious hat,
Danced on rooftops like a sprightly acrobat.
With each wobble and wiggle, oh what a sight!
He painted the town in colors so bright.

A spry little bird, with dreams to explore,
Tried surfing the breeze, till he crashed on the floor.
With a feathered grin and a flick of his wing,
He proclaimed, "I'll be back! Just wait for spring!"

A jolly old man in a polka dot coat,
Brought a bicycle made from a fine floating boat.
He pedaled through puddles, splashing with glee,
Ring, ring! said the bell, "Come join me!"

A monkey in shorts swung from tree to tree,
With ribbons and laughter, he filled the sunny spree.
Together they roamed, oh the joy was so grand,
In this whimsical world, adventure was planned.

The Spirit of the Explorer

A courageous cow set sail on a dream,
With a pirate hat and a barrel of cream.
She sought treasures hidden, oh what a thrill,
As she mooed and she swayed, on that ship, what a skill!

A rooster with swagger strutted along,
With a map in his beak, he sang quite a song.
He tripped over trinkets and giggled in jest,
"Why was I chosen? I'm simply the best!"

Then two goofy squirrels joined in the quest,
With acorns as coins, they felt truly blessed.
In a race for the cheese, they took such a dive,
"Oh look!" one exclaimed, "We're alive! We're alive!"

Under bright stars, with laughter so loud,
An unexpected friendship formed a strange crowd.
Together they danced, on the waves of delight,
A playful parade, full of joy and of light.

Maps That Lead to Destiny

A map drawn by dogs, with paws all a-flutter,
Led to a treasure of belly rubs and butter.
They howled in delight at their wiggly find,
"Let's chart a new course, leave our worries behind!"

A confused cat, with a compass askew,
Chased after a dot, a shiny bright blue.
She tumbled and spun, in a glorious whirl,
"Adventure awaits!" she gave a loud twirl.

A rabbit with glasses, so smart and precise,
Checked his map thrice, for a location that's nice.
He bounced on his feet, with a giggle and hop,
"Let's see what we find, but don't dare to stop!"

At long last they gathered, with stories galore,
From a picnic spread wide on a magical shore.
With laughter and snacks, they happily feasted,
In this journey of joy, no one ever leasted.

Echoes of Wandering Souls

A fox with a flair wore a floppy old cap,
Roamed through the woods with a twist and a flap.
He danced with the shadows, whistled a tune,
"Adventure is calling! Let's go by the moon!"

Two turtles on scooters raced down the street,
With helmets so big, they couldn't take a seat.
They laughed as they flipped, with a plop and a glide,
In the epic escapades of the great turtle ride.

A parrot in pajamas chatted away,
With tales of the sea and a colorful play.
"Squawk! We'll explore where the wild sea-frogs croak,
In search of the land where the funny hat folks."

So together they wandered, these souls full of zest,
In the realm of the silly, they felt truly blessed.
With giggles and stories that danced through the air,
Adventure was waiting, beyond all compare!

The Voyage of the Brave

With a map in my hand, I set sail,
A chicken in the pouch, my trusty ale.
Dolphins are chatting, they seem quite wise,
Yet they laugh at my shoes, oh how they criticize.

The wind sings a tune, so wild and free,
A parrot is squawking, says, "Come dance with me!"
The compass spins round, it's gone quite mental,
I'm steering through clouds, I may need a rental.

Mermaids wave warmly, with fish in their hair,
But they giggle at jelly, I swear it's not fair!
I stumble on deck, tripping over my hat,
Captain beard made of noodles - imagine that!

As night falls, the stars shiver bright,
A marzipan moon gives a sweet, silly sight.
Adventure awaits, with a wink and a cheer,
Life's a wacky voyage - now give me a beer!

A Navigator's Song

Lost in a sea of uncharted naps,
My compass is broken, it points at the snacks.
With a sandwich for treasure and soda for gold,
I'm charting a course that's decidedly bold.

The waves are just laughter, the wind blows a tease,
Sailing on pillows, oh, such a breeze!
The dolphins are plotting, I think it's a prank,
They keep drawing maps, but they're all just blank.

An octopus steers with flair and finesse,
While I try to dance in my soggy dress.
Seagulls steal cookies, they've plotted a coup,
I'm more of a sailor and less of a stew.

Yet still, I will sail for that island of fun,
Where the sun always smiles and all work is done.
So raise up your glass to the ships made of dreams,
For a journey with laughter, or so it seems!

The Essence of Adventure

Adventure's a dance where you trip then you glide,
With raccoons as dancers, I'm taken for a ride.
They wear tiny vests, like they're ready to roll,
Trying to lead me, but I'm losing control.

The mountains are wobbly, they sway side to side,
And bears in top hats join the fun with pride.
I'm lost in a forest that's oh so bizarre,
Where squirrels speak French, and they all have a car.

A bridge made of marshmallows holds strong, I can tell,
Though I sink with each step, it tastes rather swell.
With treasure on my lips and giggles in the air,
Every moment's a riddle, adventure to share.

So let's shuffle and jiggle and drink from the stream,
With friends who are zany, we'll follow our dream.
Each trip's like a party, a chat with delight,
Where fun is the essence, from morning to night!

Ascent to New Horizons

The mountain loomed, a giant beast,
We set a goal, a funny feast.
With every step, a slip or two,
Our laughter echoed, wild and true.

We packed our gear, a quirky load,
A rubber chicken, our trusty road.
The summit called, in playful tones,
With snacks and jokes, we claimed our thrones.

Each viewpoint sparked a silly cheer,
As clouds gave way, we found our steer.
With every ridge, a joke did sprout,
In this wild climb, we danced about.

At last, we waved the peak goodbye,
With goofy grins, we felt the high.
Adventure's quirks had stole the scene,
In nature's theater, we played our genes.

Bold Ventures and Lively Journeys

In search of thrills, we packed our dreams,
With mismatched socks and silly schemes.
Our map was drawn in crayon bright,
We'd find the path, come day or night.

A rickety boat, we took the chance,
With floors that creaked, we made our dance.
The fish jumped high and splashed our hats,
We burst in laughter, oh, where's the mats?

Through jungles thick and fields of glee,
We swung from vines, like wild monkeys.
With every twist, a comedic plot,
In bold ventures, we danced the lot.

As evening fell, we told our tales,
Of all the quirks, and epic fails.
With starlit skies to crown our night,
These lively journeys felt just right.

Journey Beyond the Horizon

We packed our bags for lands unknown,
With five mismatched socks and a rubber stone.
Our compass spun, like a frenzy mad,
Off we went, our spirits glad.

The train was late, the snacks were few,
In boredom's grip, we played peekaboo.
When finally we rode the rails,
We sang out loud, forgot our trails.

With every stop, a tale untold,
The people laughed, the adventures bold.
From bustling towns to fields so vast,
Our funny journey went by fast.

At sunset's glow, we waved goodbye,
With joyous hearts, we touched the sky.
Beyond horizons, where dreams expand,
In laughter's wake, we took our stand.

The Call of Uncharted Trails

With boots laced tight, we hit the road,
Each bend a mystery, a chuckle code.
Through winding paths and quirky signs,
We followed laughter as our guide defines.

A squirrel danced and stole our food,
In this mad journey, nothing was crude.
We stumbled on, with grins so wide,
The uncharted trails became our ride.

A stream to cross, our shoes would flop,
With splashes loud, we couldn't stop.
In puddles deep, we made a splash,
In muddy fun, we felt the dash.

At day's end, we shared our tales,
Of silly slips and gusty gales.
The call of trails forever rings,
In every laugh, adventure sings.

Beyond the Familiar

A sandwich kissed the ground today,
With mustard dreams all gone astray.
I tipped my cap to the grand old tree,
Who waved its branches, daring me.

A squirrel in glasses sipped some tea,
While pondering life in a sunny spree.
I joined his chat about nuts and cheese,
And both of us laughed at life's little tease.

With every step, a quirky sign,
A road that bends like a bumpy line.
I lost my map but found my grin,
As adventure's chaos pulled me in.

A dance with shadows, a twirl with fate,
The world's a circus, don't be late!
So off we go, my friends and me,
To discover joy in the strange and free.

In Search of Lost Horizons

I chased a rainbow, it slipped away,
But I found a puddle where ducks like to play.
They quacked with laughter, splashing about,
Until one stole my sandwich, without a doubt.

With goggles on, I embraced the lake,
Thought I'd meet fish, but met a mistake.
A catfish grinned, wearing a crown,
And I burst out laughing, feeling a clown.

The shore was busy with turtles in ties,
Debating the meaning of perfect pies.
I sat down to join this wise old crew,
Their wisdom was goofy, but oh so true.

With flip-flops flapping, we danced on sand,
Celebrated life in this merry land.
The sun set slowly, we cheered and spun,
In search of lost joys, we all were one.

Wild Hearts and Open Roads

A llama wore shades, cruising with flair,
In a convertible, with wind in its hair.
We chuckled together, as we zoomed past,
Crazy adventures, oh what a blast!

A raccoon with a map had plans so grand,
To find the best junk food in the land.
We followed the odors, my belly did groan,
Every snack stop turned into a throne.

We met a wise owl in search of a book,
He gave us advice with a curious look.
"Go live your dreams, but always take snacks,
And steer clear of any unfunny cracks!"

With every mile, we embraced the strange,
Life's a wild trip, oh how it can change.
We laughed at the silliness, flinging off chains,
With wild hearts and roads that never constrain.

Lanterns in the Dark

When darkness falls, my lantern glows,
Leading the way where the chuckleberry grows.
I stumbled on shadows, they danced with glee,
Whispering secrets that tickled me.

A frog in a tuxedo sang a fine tune,
Holding a garage sale under the moon.
He offered me trinkets, quite absurd,
A rubber chicken and a wobbling bird.

Bats wearing hats flew high above,
Singing sweet songs of twilight love.
I joined their chorus, quite out of key,
The night became magic, wild and free.

As lanterns flickered, we partied till dawn,
In a world where the ordinary is gone.
So here's to the night with its whimsical spark,
Together we shine, bright lanterns in the dark.

The Mysterious Quest

In lands unknown, we skipped and ran,
Chasing shadows, as only we can.
With maps drawn in crayon, oh what a sight,
Each 'X' marked treasure, or maybe a fright.

We battled a dragon made of fine fluff,
With giggles and bubbles, we'd had enough.
A quest for the ages, or just lunch at best?
Who knew the journey'd be such a jest?

Through jungles of socks and forests of toys,
We searched for the things that spark our joys.
A crown made of paper, a throne of some chairs,
We ruled our kingdom, with no time for cares.

But in the end, with a wink and a nod,
Our greatest treasure? Each laugh and each odd.
So grab your boots, let's tumble and roll,
For life is the riddle, and fun is the goal!

Footprints on New Shores

Walking on beaches with shoes made of cheese,
Leaving strange footprints, we giggle and tease.
With each step we take, we invent silly games,
As seagulls look on, wondering our names.

We built a grand castle, with moats full of goo,
Decorated with shells we found in a stew.
Crabs joined our party, with tiny crab waves,
Inviting the waves to dance and misbehave.

The tide rolled in, like a curious cat,
So we paddled away, like dogs chasing a hat.
Each splash became laughter, a chorus of fun,
As we raced the tide 'til the day was all done.

Our footprints washed away, but the memories stay,
Of silly adventures that defined our play.
On shores of imagination, we'll always explore,
Each day an epic, with laughs we adore!

The Ebb and Flow of Adventure

We woke up one morning, adventure called loud,
With waffles and syrup, we'd tackle the crowd.
Our gear was all packed, with snacks on the list,
Who knew such a day would be bursting with bliss?

We floated on puddles, equipped like a knight,
With capes made of towels, ready for flight.
The world was our canvas, we painted it bright,
Sketching our stories 'til late in the night.

Each hill we would climb, every tree that we scaled,
Was marked in our journals where laughter prevailed.
Through giggles and tumbles, the fun never ceased,
With pancakes and stories, our joy was increased.

As day turned to dusk, and we headed for home,
We promised more journeys, no reason to roam.
For in every heartbeat, every silly song,
Was the ebb and flow where we all belonged!

Routes of the Reckless

Oh, the paths we would wander, so wild and so free,
Through the woods and the fields, chanting 'Look at me!'
Our map was a scribble that made zero sense,
But our spirits were high, jumping over the fence.

We tripped on our shoelaces, tumbled and fell,
Each time we would laugh, oh, do tell, do tell!
Round every corner, we'd find a new thing,
Like a pink, polka-dotted, oversized ring.

The sun played peek-a-boo, hiding with glee,
In the wild world of wonder, just you and me.
With roots of the reckless, we danced and we swayed,
Generating stories both funny and frayed.

As night fell upon us, our tales filled the air,
Of dragons and sock monsters that lived by the bear.
Each journey together, forever will last,
In the routes of the reckless, our bright die was cast!

Exploring the Great Beyond

A llama in shades, on a mountain so high,
Dances in circles, as clouds drift by.
With socks on his hooves, oh what a sight,
He twirls through the valleys, all day and night.

A pirate on land, with a map made of cheese,
Searching for treasure amidst the tall trees.
He digs in the dirt with a fork and a knife,
Claiming his fortune, oh what a life!

A cat in a cape, with a laugh that's contagious,
Leads a parade of ducks, oh so outrageous.
Through puddles they waddle, in synchronized fun,
Splashing the locals—no time to run!

With each little journey, new tales are spun,
Adventure awaits, and it's never quite done.
So pack up your giggles, your quirks, and your style,
Join the raucous romp, stay a little while!

The Uncharted Within

Inside my own mind, a circus does bloom,
Juggling my thoughts with a vacuum and broom.
The clowns laugh and tumble, with joy they erupt,
Meanwhile my worries are all in a huddle.

A treasure map drawn with crayons in hand,
Leads me to snacks that are perfectly bland.
It's a quest for some chips and a fizzy delight,
As I navigate snacks, my heart takes to flight.

Monsters dance wildly in the shadows of doubt,
But with a good pun, I can make them all shout.
With laughter and giggles, they fade into air,
My mind's a wild fair, and I ride without care.

So here's to the journey, both silly and bright,
Exploring my psyche, oh what a delight!
Grab a comfy chair and a snack near your side,
Let's wander together, let imagination glide.

Stirred by Wandering Whispers

Whispers of wanderlust swirl in the breeze,
Tickling my ears like a sneeze that won't cease.
They sing through the trees, with a mischievous flair,
Convinced that the squirrels are plotting a dare.

With unlicensed maps and a backpack of dreams,
I set off for wonders that sparkle and beam.
A toad in a top hat offers me tea,
"Join us," he beckons, "Come frolic and flee!"

A shadowy path with giggles unheard,
Leads to a garden where laughter is stirred.
The flowers are singing, each one a delight,
I dance through their petals, all day and all night.

As twilight approaches, I follow a star,
That guides me to shores where the giggles are far.
With friends made anew, beneath skies oh so wide,
Together we journey, let's wander, let's ride!

The Flame of Discoveries

A spark in the heart, igniting the fun,
Chasing after dreams like a pizza on the run.
With each lovely mishap and stumble I take,
I gather sweet stories like frosting on cake.

Through jungles of jellybeans, I roam with glee,
While marshmallow bears hold a banquet for me.
They toast with their s'mores, so gooey and loud,
A feast full of laughter beneath a bright cloud.

A parade of adventures pops up on the way,
From dancing high mountains to splashes in bay.
I twirl with the dolphins, and slide down a slide,
When joy is the treasure, I'm buzzing inside.

So let's fuel this flame with our quirkiest plots,
Together in laughter, we'll connect all the dots.
With every new venture, the spark starts to glow,
And off to new worlds of pure whimsy we go!

Dreams Woven with Courage

With laces tied and pockets stuffed,
We march ahead with hearts quite puffed.
Each step we take, a laugh or two,
While dodging pigeons, who knew they'd stew?

We'll scale the peaks and tumble down,
In capes of courage, we don't wear a frown.
With marshmallow clouds all up above,
We gaze in wonder, wrapped in love.

So here's to schemes that make us grin,
With silly hats we wear with sin.
Each blunder's gold, a treasure bright,
As we dance with chance in the moonlight.

In dreams we chase, absurd, no doubt,
With ice cream trails, we'll twist about.
Through every stumble, joy's the creed,
In laughter's wake, we plant the seed.

Through the Eyes of a Voyager

A map upside down, oh what a sight,
We set our course with giggles and fright.
In whirlwinds of breadcrumbs, we find our way,
As squirrels debate if it's picnic day.

With every wrong turn, a story grows,
In rubber boots, splashing through the snows.
We barter with ducks, for tales of the tide,
While donning our smiles, nothing to hide.

The stars in the sky wink their cheeky names,
While we play hide and seek with our silly games.
With hiccups of joy, we chase the sun,
Even tangled in vines, it's all just fun.

So we raise our glasses, filled to the brim,
Toast to the mishaps, let's sing or swim.
In the heart of our journeys, wild and bright,
Adventure awaits, and it feels just right.

Where the Compass Leads

With a compass spinning, we take the leap,
Unruly laughter is ours to keep.
Through marshy lands where the gremlins stomp,
And giggly trolls give a cheeky chomp.

We'll dance with shadows, make friends with gnomes,
Find treasure in junk, and claim it as homes.
With our heads in clouds and feet in mud,
Each moment a whirl, oh what a flood!

Pinecone hats flopping on heads so proud,
We howl at the moon, shout, "Let's be loud!"
With every wrong guess, a story to weave,
In the land of make-believe, we don't grieve.

Through fields of daisies where laughter's the key,
And chases of whimsy feel like a spree.
With sprinkles of joy, we carve our path,
Adventure awaits, let's share a good laugh!

The Dance of Serendipity

Dance in the rain, with umbrellas gone,
We sway to the tunes of a cheeky con.
Skip past the worries, twirl with delight,
Each twist and turn sets our hearts alight.

We stumble on treasures, old coins and a shoe,
Imagining stories of what they once knew.
With bushes as taxis, we ride with flair,
And laugh at the squirrels who've lost their hair.

Each dance step a leap, follow the breeze,
As giggles escape with the greatest of ease.
Through garden mazes, adventure unfolds,
With lemons for gold, and riches untold.

So let's spin and whirl 'neath the vibrant skies,
Embracing the chaos and wild surprise.
With every stumble, we discover new cheer,
In this dance of fortune, our hearts persevere.

Escapes Beyond the Horizon

With a suitcase full of socks,
And a map that's upside down,
We'll sail on cardboard boats,
To the land of Giggle Town.

A compass that points to lunch,
And a seagull on a quest,
We dive into the sea of fun,
Forgetting what we know best.

Pirates made of jelly beans,
Dance around with silly glee,
While we sail with squeaky shoes,
Through waves of laughter and tea.

Under skies of rainbow stripes,
We twirl in circles, feeling grand,
Adventure's waiting everywhere,
So come and join this zany band.

The Mapmaker's Dreams

A map that leads to candy lands,
With chocolate rivers flowing,
Ice cream mountains, cloud-topped peaks,
And a breeze that keeps on blowing.

Each line's a silly riddle,
In sketched-out doodles bright,
Follow the dots of giggles,
Into the silly night.

Misshaped kingdoms, curvy roads,
With roads made out of cheese,
Navigation through a game of tags,
Beneath the dancing trees.

Each marking brings a chuckle,
To the land where fun's supreme,
So grab your crayons, let's explore,
And dive into this dream.

Wandering Feet

With shoes that squeak like mice,
And socks that dare to clash,
We chase adventure's joyful spark,
In a wild and wobbly dash.

Every step a giggle,
As we twirl and spin around,
With feet that tap and tango,
On this merry, crazy ground.

Paths that lead to crazy places,
Where the grass grows upside down,
We'll wander into wonder,
And wear the silliest crown.

So come join the hopping gang,
Let's tread where laughter's free,
With wandering feet and happy hearts,
We'll dance through life with glee.

Wild Heart

With a heart that leaps like rabbits,
And a grin that shines like gold,
We tumble through the fields of dreams,
With stories yet untold.

Each day's a new surprise,
As we chase the clouds away,
With wild hearts, we can conquer,
All the silliness at play.

Bouncing like a kangaroo,
Finding treasures in the dirt,
Every blunder turns to laughter,
In the fanciest of shirts.

No map can hold this spirit,
Nor cage this joyful beat,
With wild hearts, we'll roam the world,
And dance on every street.

A Tale of Uncharted Roads

On roads that twist like pretzels,
And signs that are all wrong,
We'll sing the songs of travelers,
As we wander all day long.

With backpacks stuffed with giggles,
And snacks that make us cheer,
We conquer every lap and curve,
With silly hats and beer.

Each turn reveals a wonder,
As we trip on flowers bright,
In a land where fun is common,
And every wrong feels right.

So grab your map of mischief,
Let's roam where laughter grows,
For every step's a story,
On these wild, uncharted roads.

Stars as Our Guide

Under the glow of a twinkling sky,
We dance with shadows, oh my, oh my!
With maps upside down and cups half full,
We stumble on laughter and wonder, oh cool!

The stars play tricks on our merry heads,
Leading us onward to outlandish beds.
We find a sandwich that's lost in time,
And laugh as it waltzes, a true mime!

Our compass spins like a wild old cat,
Chasing our tails, oh imagine that!
With each silly step, a treasure unfolds,
We gather giggles like stories retold.

Through goofy plots and curious bends,
We sketch our journey with zany pens.
For fun's the ticket, wherever we roam,
In the chaos of stars, we've found our home.

Trails of Twilight

As twilight whispers, we hurry along,
Chasing the fireflies that hum a song.
With shoes tied backward and socks on wrong,
We dive into mishaps where we all belong.

A squirrel steals snacks while we pose for a grin,
Leaving us chuckling through thick and thin.
With every misstep, our spirits lift high,
In the dance of the evening, we learn to fly!

The owls hoot softly, quoting silly quotes,
While we search for treasure aboard rubber boats.
With giggles arising from dusk's gentle fold,
Each trail we wander turns into pure gold.

We'll never fit in with a serious crew,
For laughter's our compass, that much is true.
As twilight beckons with shadows to play,
We happily frolic until break of day.

The Art of Exploration

With a map in hand and a wink in our eyes,
We plan our escape to the land of surprise.
On bicycles painted in every hue,
We pedal past pondering, giggling like dew.

The world is our canvas, watch us create,
With splashes of joy, we celebrate fate.
Each corner reveals a pop-up parade,
We join the silliness, not afraid to invade!

We find a lost shoe, a cartoonish prize,
And wear it with pride, oh what a surprise!
With every odd object that crosses our path,
We wear our creations; just feel the math!

From puddles to pranks, our journey just flows,
With the sun as our partner and giggles that grow.
In this art of exploring, we paint our own fable,
Crafted in laughter, forever unstable.

Discovering Forgotten Realms

In the attic of dreams, we find dusty chests,
Filled with odd trinkets and quirky quests.
With goggles and capes, we're ready to dive,
Into realms where the impossible comes alive!

We meet a fine dragon who bakes us a pie,
And dances with unicorns under the sky.
In clouds made of candy and rivers of cheese,
We skip through the magic, oh what a tease!

The clocks tick backward, now isn't that fun?
As we trip over time, our adventures have begun.
In forests of giggles, we tumble and roll,
Exploring forgotten realms, heart and soul.

With maps that are scribbled and riddles to solve,
We treasure each moment, eagerly evolve.
For in every corner of wonder's embrace,
We find the joy of this whimsical chase.

Journey's Gracious Embrace

A squirrel in a beret, oh what a sight,
He dances on branches, such pure delight.
With acorns for maracas, he knows the tune,
A furry maestro shall serenade the moon.

The raccoons bring snacks in a fancy box,
They party all night, wearing mismatched socks.
With laughter they tumble, and spill the wine,
In the wild's grand gala, they're feeling divine.

A bird with a monocle reads the news,
Declares it's a day for sugar and blues.
"Let's soar to the clouds, with cake for a treat!"
They hire a pig in a suit for the feat.

So here's to the whimsy that stalks through the trees,
To creatures in costumes, swaying with ease.
Adventure awaits with a comedic stunt,
In the forest of fun, let's join the front!

Paths of Potential

A penguin in flip-flops waltzes with glee,
On paths paved with giggles, where none can foresee.
He slips and he slides with a flair so unique,
Any step in this venture is sure to be sleek.

A cat on a bicycle rides with such grace,
In a top hat adorned with a popcorn embrace.
He rings the bell loudly, oh what a display,
This whimsical journey will surely make your day.

A turtle in sneakers zooms past in a blur,
While critters all cheer, "What a speedy old fur!"
He laughs in response while spinning about,
Adventure unfolds with a jump and a shout.

They dance through the meadow, these characters bright,
With rules made of laughter, they frolic in light.
Each twist in the tale leads to giggling delight,
In paths filled with promise, the future feels right!

Unspooling the Map of Dreams

A moose with a compass is lost on the trail,
He's searching for treasures but finds a big snail.
"Excuse me, dear sir, have you seen my way?"
The snail just shrugs and continues to sway.

An octopus artist paints landscapes quite grand,
With seven bright brushes and a slippery hand.
He swirls and he twirls in colorful streams,
Creating a world born from unfathomable dreams.

A llama dons goggles as he sails the skies,
With a wink and a nod, he's ready to rise.
"Adventure awaits in the clouds up above,"
He shouts to his friends, "Let's find what we love!"

So here's to the journey, wherever they roam,
With laughter and mishaps, they're never alone.
Maps unspool in chaos, the winds of delight,
In the laughter of dreams, they ignite the night!

Chasing the Wind

A dog in a tutu runs after a breeze,
He twirls and he spins, with such playful ease.
His paws in the air, he leaps to the beat,
In a chase for the wind, life can't be beat.

A cat with a kite rides the gusts overhead,
Laughing at clouds, "You're no match for my thread!"
With laughter in tow, they float high above,
In the theatre of skies, they dance with a shove.

A raccoon with a diary scrawls tales of fun,
Of mischief and mayhem and pranks by the sun.
He shares with the stars as the night starts to sway,
In the chase of the wind, they've lost track of day.

So join in the frolic, the whirl and the spin,
With dreams made of laughter, let the wildness begin.
In the jubilation where we all must descend,
What pleasures await in this chasing of wind!

Journey into the Unknown

A llama in shades, on a skateboard,
Zooms past the trees, what a bold hoard!
With marshmallows tossed in the air,
Who knew adventure could be so rare?

Bouncing across the marshy bog,
A frog in a tux, like a fancy dog.
He jumps through puddles, splashes with glee,
Singing a tune that's catchy, you see!

The map is upside down, or so I think,
It leads us to a fountain, filled with pink drink!
We dance like penguins, arms in the sky,
As passersby chuckle and wonder why.

So here we go, with a laugh and a cheer,
To ride a unicycle, with laughter near!
With a squirrel as sidekick, what could go wrong?
At least we'll have fun, all day long!

Whispers of the Wind's Path

A breeze tickles my nose, oh what a tease,
It whispers sweet secrets, with laughter and ease.
A raccoon with a bowtie, dances in style,
Says 'Join me, dear friend, let's prance for a mile!'

Clouds shaped like sandwiches float overhead,
While jellybeans tumble from a sky that's well-fed.
Two turtles race by on a skateboard so grand,
Chasing the sun, it's the best holiday planned!

With a wink and a nod, the shadows all play,
A merry-go-round made of cheese on display.
We twirl and we spin till we can't catch our breath,
As the breeze keeps on giggling, holding back death!

The path is a puzzle, with laughter untold,
Every step brings a chuckle, more joy to behold.
So let's toss our worries up to the trees,
And ride with the whispers, all carried by breeze!

The Call of Daring Daydreams

A dragon in pajamas flies through the sky,
With cupcakes for wings, oh my, oh my!
We ride on marshmallows, fluffy and sweet,
Chasing down candy canes for a treat.

Balloons in a parade dance from the street,
With octopus drummers tapping their feet.
Each note is a giggle, a call to the brave,
Adventure's sweet song is the laughter we crave.

The moon wears a crown made of sparkling light,
As we host a circus under the night.
Clowns juggle pickles while poodles do tricks,
What a wacky world, full of silly flicks!

So grab your best buddy, let's leap and we'll hop,
On roller skates winding till we flop!
With daring daydreams, we'll conquer it all,
In this wild realm where silliness calls!

Beneath the Starlit Sky

Under a sky with a wink and a twinkle,
A snail in a parka starts to skedaddle.
With garden gnomes giggling in tussled cheer,
Even the night critters can't hide their sneer.

A cat wearing glasses reads tales of delight,
Of pirates who only knew how to kite.
They sailed on a pizza, what a sight to behold,
As stars burst with laughter, stories unfold!

A raccoon with a monocle leads the parade,
With all of the bunnies in hats that they made.
They stomp through the grass with a jump and a yip,
In the moonlight's glow, it's a comical trip!

So here we shall stay, beneath twinkling dreams,
Where skies dance with stories and laughter redeems.
For every adventure is wrapped in a smile,
As we bounce to the rhythm, mile after mile!

The Heart's Expedition

In boots too big and socks that slide,
We set our course with woeful pride.
A map that's drawn in crayon blue,
Leads us to who knows where, it's true.

Our compass spins, we've lost the plot,
With snacks to munch, we're tied in knots.
The treasure's gold? Just chocolate bars,
We laugh and dance beneath the stars.

With every step, we chase a dream,
In tangled woods, we hear a scream.
"Is that a bear or just a cat?"
Adventure calls, "Now where you at?"

So here's to quests both grand and small,
In lands where silly stories sprawl.
Raise your glasses, join the cheer,
For journeys wild, we've nothing to fear.

Secrets of the Untamed

In jungles deep where monkeys chatter,
We swat at bugs, and what's the matter?
With every step, we find a clue,
Is that a bush or something new?

We searched for gold, but found a shoe,
Whose is it? Who knows what to do?
A riddle lost in tangled vines,
We stumble here, and laugh in lines.

The trees dance wildly, leaves in flight,
As we declare, "We'll rule the night!"
But tripping on our silly feet,
We end up with a laughing treat.

So gather 'round, adventurers brave,
In wild places, come out and wave.
The secrets here are goofy too,
With every turn, an "Oops!" or two.

Tides of Adventure

The ocean's wide, we grab our gear,
But why's the water coming near?
With surfboards made of cardboard sheets,
We paddle out to face our feats.

A dolphin jumps, it gives a cheer,
While seagulls squawk and flit so near.
But here we are, feeling quite lost,
In wave upon wave, what's the cost?

Our boat is sinking, don't lose hope!
We're marooned now, a funny trope.
With coconuts we craft a throne,
And laugh aloud, we're never alone.

So ride the waves, oh brave and bold,
In salty air, let stories unfold.
With a splash and giggle, embrace the day,
For life's great fun, come what may.

Unwritten Chapters

In dusty books with tales untold,
We turn the pages, feeling bold.
With sticky notes and doodles bright,
We write our dreams under the light.

A dragon snorts, it breathes blue flame,
While knights on bicycles play the game.
Through forests strange, we roam and race,
Creating worlds, we find our place.

But wait, what's that? A plot twist here,
A talking cat is now our peer.
We cackle loud, with glee we shout,
In every line, adventure's sprout.

So pen in hand, we craft our fate,
With laughter loud, we celebrate.
In journeys wild and stories grand,
Together still, hand in hand.

Navigating Life's Wilderness

In the woods we stumbled, what a sight,
A raccoon in a jacket, oh what a fright.
He waved at us, twirling his cane,
We burst out laughing, going insane.

We tried to follow well-worn paths,
But ended up drawing the forest's wrath.
With branches scratching our silly hats,
We danced like fools, just like the spats.

Lost in the thicket, we made a map,
With doodles of squirrels and a bear's nap.
As twilight approached, we chose to stray,
To find our way home, we'll just ballet.

Through tangled vines and underbrush green,
We led our crew with the grace of a queen.
A nature trip, what a crazy trip,
Next time we'll bring a GPS and sip.

Shifting Sands of Exploration

On sandy dunes, we rode our boards,
With tube socks on, striking flailing chords.
The camels giggled; how absurd we looked,
We chased them around, feeling all hooked.

Launching ourselves like popcorn in the air,
Our friends built castles without a care.
We toppled the towers, a playful attack,
Sandy saboteurs on a laughing track.

The sun set low, the sky ablaze,
We slid down hills, lost in a daze.
Wiping our faces, we all agreed,
Next year we'll come with sunscreen indeed!

The glittery dunes held our giggles tight,
As night rolled in, it felt just right.
Stories shared of our goofy spree,
In this wild land, forever carefree.

Glimpses of Daring Days

In a pirate ship made from cardboard boxes,
We sailed across puddles, dodging the foxes.
With cutlasses drawn, and hats askew,
We claimed the neighborhood, 'Tis Pirate Crew!

We spoke in tongues, a language so grand,
'Arr matey!' echoing across the land.
But one quick turn left us in stitches,
The captain fell in, saying 'I have it switched!'

With bandanas flying, we searched for loot,
Found candy wrappers—that's quite astute.
The blazing sun turned our cheeks so red,
Yet laughter held strong; adventure ahead.

As twilight crept in, we pondered our fate,
To be landlubbers now? Oh, what a fate!
We packed up our dreams, however surreal,
And vowed to set sail again—what a deal!

Vanguard of the Venture

We donned our gear with flair and style,
Approaching the mountain, we flashed a smile.
With snacks strapped on and water too,
Who knew climbing would feel like the zoo?

The path twisted crazy, with rocks here and there,
One slipped and tumbled, oh what a scare!
Wobbling upwards like newborn deer,
We conquered our fears, fueled by cheer.

We sang off-key, a tune quite absurd,
A chorus of giggles, not one day blurred.
True mountain goats, we laughed through the aches,
With blisters and bruises, but we won't break!

As we reached the top, great views we faced,
A selfie we snapped, no moment replaced.
So here's to the fun, the stumbles, the falls,
On this wild excursion, we answered the calls!

Footprints in the Dust of Dreams

In slippers I roam, through fields of delight,
Chasing shadows of laughter, from morning till night.
I step on the clouds, with penguins as pals,
They waddle and giggle, like mischievous gals.

The sun plays a tune, as I dance with the stars,
My spaceship's a cookie, with a side of guitars.
Flying high on a kite, with ambitions that soar,
I land in a cupcake, and yearn for some more.

The rabbits are writing, in crayon and ink,
Their poetry's wild, always making me think.
I follow the breadcrumbs, on paths full of twists,
With cupcakes for lanterns, I can't resist.

Oh, footprints of whimsy, in dust they will lay,
Guide me to treasures where giggles can play.
Adventures will tickle, with joy like a dream,
In a world full of wonder, or so it would seem.

Navigating the Unfamiliar

With a map made of jelly, I set off to roam,
Through marshmallow mountains, I call it my home.
I ask silly seagulls for directions that change,
They flap and they cackle, which drives me quite strange.

Down rivers of lemonade, on boats made of toast,
I sail with my friends, from coast to warm coast.
We fish for ideas, with nets made of cheese,
While giant ants play chess, with giggles and wheezes.

The compass spins wildly, a laugh in disguise,
Leading us straight to an octopus's pies.
With silly confetti, we dance on the shores,
While crabs in tuxedos knock on welcome doors.

Oh, navigating this whimsy, with courage and cheer,
Each turn brings a grin, as we conquer our fear.
In a world that is twisted, yet full of delight,
We'll map out our dreams, till we fly out of sight.

Stories in the Breath of the Breeze

The breeze whispers secrets, of yonder and here,
With tales from the daisies who giggle in cheer.
They flutter their petals, and dance in the air,
While squirrels play poker, without a care.

A dragon named Fred, with a hat made of cheese,
Invites me for tea, with chocolate chip peas.
He spins yarns of travel, on spoons made of gold,
Of mountains that giggle and rivers that scold.

With whispers of wonders, the wind tends to bend,
With laughter that sparkles, like stars in the end.
I sit in a hammock, made from wild glee,
While clouds drop down stories for you and for me.

In the breath of the breeze, where nonsense is king,
Each tale spins a giggle, like a round of spring.
So come take a ride, on this whimsical breeze,
Where stories are wild, and laughter's a tease.

The Heart's Quest for Wonder

With a skip and a hop, my heart leads the way,
To lands filled with laughter and vibrant bouquet.
Where flowers wear glasses, and frogs sing in tune,
And pizza grows on trees, under a savory moon.

A quest for the silly, with socks on my hands,
I journey through jungles of gumdrop lands.
Where each friendly cactus has jokes up its sleeve,
And fairies play tag, so fast you wouldn't believe.

Through valleys of giggles, my heart starts to sway,
With balloons made of chocolate, it's hard not to stay.
I chase after wishes that float by like boats,
While unicorns serenade in shimmering coats.

On this quest for the wonder, where fun is the prize,
Each step brings a chuckle, and joy multiplies.
So come join the frolic, with cheer in your chest,
In a world full of whimsy, we'll follow our quest.

Adventurer's Spirit

With a pack and a map, I set out today,
Chasing trails that lead me far away.
A left turn, a right, then a tumble and roll,
My journey begins in a gopher's hole.

Climbing up mountains, I slip on a stone,
Only to land on a cactus, alone.
I chuckle and laugh, what a sight to behold,
My spirit is bright even when I'm cold.

A river I cross, with a leap and a splash,
My socks are now wet - what a dandy clash!
But who needs dry feet on a quest so bold?
This is the joy that adventure unfolds.

As sunset arrives, I sit on the shore,
With fireflies dancing, I start to snore.
Tomorrow brings more, oh what a delight,
In a world full of wonders, I'll sleep tight tonight.

Odyssey of the Heart

In a world of unknowns, I follow my beat,
With a dance like a wild child, can't stay off my feet.
A compass gone rogue, spins round with a fling,
I'm lost, but it feels like I'm chasing a king.

Through forests of giggles and valleys of cheer,
I whimper at shadows that sneak up near.
But with snacks in my pocket, I conquer my fear,
For adventure is sweet, and laughter is here.

An orange that rolled down a hill just for fun,
Chasing my dinner was not the right run.
Yet with each goofy blunder, a tale unfolds,
Where the journey is richer than treasures of gold.

So raise a glass (of juice) to the whimsy of life,
For every odd moment can cut through the strife.
With a heart full of courage, and cheer as my chart,
I'll dance through each day on this odyssey of heart.

Soaring Where Few Have Gone

On a bicycle built for two, we zoom down the track,
With a squeaky old horn and a bag full of snacks.
We pedal through clouds like a bird in the sky,
Who knew all this fun would come with a pie?

Up hills and down dales, then into a tree,
Our laughter rings clear, it feels wild and free.
A squirrel yells 'hello!' as we walk by the gate,
He thinks we're the weirdest; we think it's just fate.

With sun in our eyes, we wander and roam,
Every twist and each turn feels like coming back home.
The wind is our friend, it gives us a shove,
Soaring up high, in our journey of love.

Each adventure we share paints a saga so grand,
As we leap through the air, with the world in a hand.
And where few have soared, we're just getting started,
In a field of pure laughter, our spirits unguarded.

The Echo of Distant Lands

From mountaintops high, I let out a yell,
It echoes back 'Whoo!' like a curious spell.
I laugh with the valleys, I sing to the streams,
In a world full of wonders, I'm living my dreams.

A donkey in sandals brings humor so light,
It sways as it struts, such a comical sight.
I chuckle and stamp, for the fun never ends,
In the rhythm of travel, even time bends.

With spoons as my drums, I march through the town,
Spinning tales to those who're feeling quite down.
The echo of laughter, a melody grand,
Is the heartbeat of places where few really stand.

So here's to the journeys, the laughter and cheer,
With every new step, let's draw adventure near.
For in distant lands, where laughter's a thread,
The echoes of joy will forever be spread.

A Feathered Dream

Upon my head, a bird did land,
In bright red feathers, oh so grand!
I tipped my cap, it gave a nod,
And off it flew, like a little god.

With every flap, my worries flew,
In its wake, a feathery brew.
I chased it down, oh what a sight,
A dance of joy in morning light.

A stolen treat from my lunch box,
That feathery thief, a clever fox!
We shared a giggle, me and the bird,
A silly tale, absurdly absurd!

So here's to adventures in the skies,
With birds and laughs as my surprise.
In dreams we glide, in fun we play,
Each feathered wander brings a new day!

Unraveled by the Wind

A gust of breeze, my hat took flight,
Spinning round like a silly kite.
I chased it down, through puddles and grime,
Wishing I had planned for this crime!

It danced on roofs, it twirled on poles,
Like a mischievous spirit with playful goals.
I laughed and shouted, "Come back here!",
But it zoomed away without a fear.

Through gardens bright, and streets so wide,
I found new friends in the hat's wild ride.
With every tumble, a giggle grew,
As I raced to catch that floppy blue.

Finally it landed, on a dog's head!
I joined the laughter, the joy widespread.
For in every story of chase and fray,
Life's twists and turns lead us astray!

Beneath the Starlit Sky

Beneath the stars, we made a pact,
To journey forth, no looking back.
Our hats atop, with feathers bright,
We twirled and danced through the starry night.

With every step, our laughter soared,
Each silly joke, a joy restored.
We tripped and stumbled, lost in glee,
In moonlight's glow, we felt so free.

A comet dashed, with a wink and a whirl,
We cheered and laughed, what a twirl!
Under the cosmos, we spun around,
Joyful echoes of silly sound.

In dreams we set our hearts ablaze,
With every star, we painted phases.
So here's to nights when laughter flies,
Beneath the vast and twinkling skies!

The Thrill of the Unknown

We packed our bags, no map in hand,
To find the fun in mystery land.
With snacks and giggles, we hit the road,
Each corner turned, a new episode!

A sign that says, "This way to Waffles!"
A wild detour, no time for scoffles!
We laughed so hard, we nearly cried,
As syrup rivers took us for a ride.

Through fields of daisies, we skipped and ran,
With every step, we formed our plan.
To follow whims, to chase delight,
In a world where every turn feels right.

So join the ride, embrace the fun,
For life's a game, and we've just begun.
With hats a-flapping, let's take our chance,
In the thrill of the unknown, let's dance!

Banners of the Bold

In the land where the llamas stroll,
A brave knight shouts like a toddler's goal,
With banners that flap high in the breeze,
He trips on his cape, oh, such a tease!

Coconuts fall from tropical trees,
As pirate parrots squawk with ease,
Our hero skips like a dance floor queen,
Waving his sword, what a sight to be seen!

The treasure map drawn with crayon right,
Leads him to snacks, what a tasty bite!
With every misstep, he laughs and spins,
Chasing the cat where the adventure begins!

In the realm of the clumsy and fun,
Every mishap is a victory won,
So here's to the bold in their silly quest,
In laughter and joy, they find their best!

The Spirit of Exploration

In a boat made of marshmallows, we sail,
With gummy bears as our hearty crew trail,
The captain sneezes, what a sight it is,
The wind's blown away his cereal fizz!

We navigate through hot chocolate streams,
Dodging giant cookies, oh, what sweet dreams!
With spoons for oars and sprinkles galore,
Each sprinkle we scoop, we search for more!

But the treasure's not gold, oh no, not fate,
It's the laughter we share, oh, isn't that great?
As we tumble and bounce, the world feels right,
In our silly adventures, we shine so bright!

So grab your friends, let's set sail today,
With giggles and joy, we'll laugh all the way,
For in the heart of the quest we find,
The spirit of fun is the greatest kind!

Echoes of Distant Shores

On distant shores where the crabs can dance,
A pirate sings of his last romance,
With a wooden leg that clinks like a bell,
He tips his hat, quite the sight to compel!

A mermaid giggles, her tail in a twist,
As dolphins join in, none could resist,
With flippers flapping, they leap in the air,
Creating bubbles, swirling everywhere!

But alas! The punchline comes with a splash,
The pirate slips on a clam, what a crash!
With laughter that echoes across the blue,
Together, we share a whimsical view!

So raise up your drinks made of sea foam,
To journeys and laughter far away from home,
For each wave brings tales of funny delight,
In watches of sun and the mister of night!

Unraveled in the Wild

In the forest where the squirrels plot,
An explorer thinks he has found quite a lot,
With a map upside down and compass on pause,
He's tracking a squirrel with a shiny pink claw!

His gear is a mismatched jumble for sure,
With a spoon for a hat and shoes made of fur,
He wanders in circles, oh, how he strides,
Chasing a shadow that simply derides!

The trees seem to giggle, the rocks have their say,
As he trips over roots in a most clumsy way,
But every new tumble raises up delight,
For laughter lives wild under the moonlight!

So raise up your canteen filled with sweet tea,
To the joy of the journey, oh, wild and free,
For in each misstep and silly mischief,
We find the true treasure, pure and not stiff!

www.ingramcontent.com/pod-product-compliance
Lightning Source LLC
Chambersburg PA
CBHW070303120526
44590CB00017B/2549